Winter
THE AUSTRALIAN SHEPHERD WITHOUT A TAIL

Amy Curran

Dedication

For Simone, an inspiring young lady who adores her Australian Shepherds, and who is exceptionally beautiful on the inside and out.

Love Amy and Tracey x

WINTER: THE AUSTRALIAN SHEPHERD WITH NO TAIL
ISBN: 978-0-6482393-6-9
A Tales of Tails Early Reader

Published in Australia by
PINK COFFEE PUBLISHING
PO Box 483, Oberon NSW 2787
www.pinkcoffeepublishing.com

Text and Illustrations Copyright Amy Curran 2018
All Rights Reserved

National Library of Australia Cataloguing-in-Publication entry information can be found at www.nla.gov.au

Photo of Simone courtesy Di Watson Photography

Contents

Chaper One   5
Chapter Two   10
Chapter Three   17
Chapter Four   23
Chapter Five   31
Chapter Six   35
Chapter Seven   42

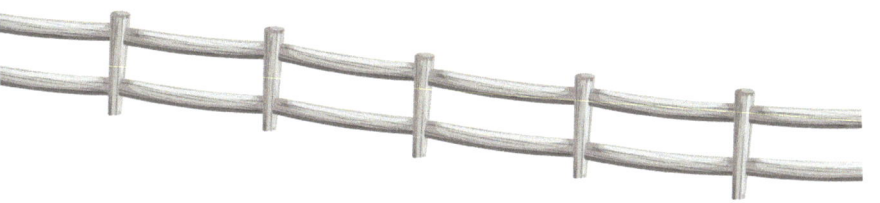

A guide to EARLY READER levels

A first reader, short sentences and limited amount of text on each page.
Less than 750 words.
Age range to 6 years old.

Sentences become a little longer, and paragraphs are introduced. Bigger words.
Less than 1500 words.
Age range to 8 years old.

These books are for readers ready to be independent. Contain Chapters, and more complex words.
Age range to 10 years old.

The level of each book can be identified by the number, and colour of the banner, on the cover.

Chapter One

Winter was a gorgeous Australian Shepherd. She was the most beautifully coloured dog anyone had ever seen. Her coat was an intricate patchwork of blue, grey and black, and she had bright copper points on her face and legs. Her soft white chest was just perfect for a cosy hug.

Winter lived on a farm with lots of other dogs, a couple of cats and many, many horses. The horses that lived on the farm were interesting colours as well, and Winter loved hiding amongst them in the paddocks.

The horses on the farm were Quarter Horses. That doesn't mean they were only part of a horse though! That was their breed, and they were many different colours.

Winter's favourite horse was Blue Valentine, but everyone just called him Old Blue. He was a blue roan colour, gorgeous just like Winter.

Winter loved the adventures that she went on with Old Blue. Every weekend, they would head off to a competition in another town, always somewhere different.

Old Blue would ride in the trailer, and Winter would ride in the truck with Buster.

Buster was a nice man. He looked after Old Blue and Winter very well.

Chapter Two

The weekend came, and an early start signalled to Winter that they were off on another great adventure somewhere. Buster came into the barn and put Old Blue's travel boots on.

When she got excited, her bottom would wriggle so fast! It always made Old Blue whinny. He thought she was very funny.

Buster loaded up Old Blue into the trailer, and Winter jumped up into the truck.

Off they went, through the sweeping bends in the road, past the National Park where the giant Sequoia trees were and down alongside the lake.

Winter started to get sleepy. The bends in the road always made her sleepy.

Winter was woken by the truck coming to a stop. She got up and looked out of her window.

Wow!

This was a big competition, bigger than others they had been to. There were horses everywhere, so many colours, but none like Old Blue.

She bounced out of the truck door that Buster had left open, and bounded around to see Old Blue.

Buster was putting some straw into the stall for Old Blue.

He would always make sure Winter and Old Blue were comfortable before he looked after himself.

Chapter Three

Winter sat patiently near the stall while she waited for Buster to come back. He had gone to get his competition number. The riders wore these so their scores could be recorded easily. She loved watching the horses go past and would tilt her head if she saw one that looked especially interesting.

"Hey!"

Winter jumped. She didn't know where the voice had come from.

"You! Over here!"

The voice had come from behind the announcer's box. Winter bounded over to see who was there.

As she turned around the side of the box, a group of dogs started laughing loudly. They did not stop.

Winter wondered what they were laughing at.

She wanted to know what the joke was as well so she could have fun and laugh with them.

"Oh, wow! She really doesn't have one!" one of the dogs laughed.

"I told you!" another said, rolling around.

Winter tilted her head. She was very confused.

"What are you laughing at?" she asked.

"Your tail! Where is it?" the black and white dog managed to say in between his crazy laughter.

All of the other dogs seemed to laugh even louder.

Winter realised they were laughing at her. She was so sad.

She turned around and wandered back to Old Blue's stall.

Chapter Four

Winter wanted to tell Old Blue all about the mean dogs, how they had laughed at her and teased her. But she couldn't. Old Blue was there to ride in the competition. She couldn't distract him with her problems.

Buster finished saddling up and hopped on top of Old Blue.

"Come on, Winter," Buster said. "Come and watch us from the gate."

Winter really didn't want to go back near the other dogs again. The gate was right near the announcer's box where they had been before. But she always watched Old Blue, and she could not let him down, so she followed behind.

She tried to hide behind Old Blue so the other dogs wouldn't see her. Old Blue was wondering why she was so close to his tail. It was making him walk funny because he didn't want to accidentally knock her. It was hard for her to see where she was going too, but she didn't want to be laughed at again.

They reached the gate, and Winter found a spot beside the arena, out of the way where she hoped the other dogs wouldn't see her.

Buster and Old Blue went into the arena in front of the judges. There were so many people in the stands around the arena. They all cheered as Old Blue entered.

Buster and Old Blue were a great team. They were known as one of the best steer roping teams around.

Old Blue was so fast out of the barrier he looked like a blue flash, and today he was as fast as ever.

The barrier was dropped, and Old Blue bolted out after the steer. Buster swung his rope and hooked the steer's horns straight away.

The crowd cheered.

Winter got excited too. She tilted her head to each side as Buster jumped down and pulled the steer to the ground.

Suddenly, while Winter was distracted, the other dogs appeared behind her. They let out a huge laugh, and the noise shocked her so much that she rolled out into the arena.

At that moment, Old Blue was cantering around the arena. A look of shock came over his face as he tried desperately to stop in time.

Winter sat up stunned. She had nowhere to go! She had to get out of his way. She couldn't go back to the side of the arena where the mean dogs were.

She wasn't fast enough to run forwards …

Chapter Five

Winter was not sure how she did it, and neither was Old Blue. It was all a bit of a blur to Winter, but apparently, as Old Blue got closer he leaned in to her, and she had leapt up onto his back, right up onto his saddle.

It was the only place she could have gone to avoid Old Blue running over her, not being able to stop in time.

The crowd went wild in amazement.

Winter sat proudly on top of Old Blue as the crowd continued to cheer.

Buster was just as surprised but happier to see that Winter was okay.

Buster led Old Blue out of the arena while Winter stayed in the saddle.

She was so happy!

It felt so good to see the world from up so high too.

As they walked around the side of the announcer's box, the other dogs were all in a line, their mouths open.

"Ah, congratulations there, lass," one of them said to her. He looked embarrassed.

"Yeah, some riding you did there!" another dog said.

Winter smiled.

Chapter Six

Later that afternoon, the riders were called to gather in the arena for the presentation.

Old Blue stayed in his stall having a rest. Winter went down with Buster to the arena, hopeful that they had got a good score.

When they got to the gate, Winter stopped and waited to the side while Buster continued on.

The announcer's loud voice called the scores and announced the winners as "Buster Lambert and Blue Valentine!"

The crowd went wild.

"There is another part of this combination, though, I must include," the announcer said. "That blue dog over there, what's her name?" He looked at Buster.

"That's my dog Winter," Buster replied proudly.

"A mighty fine dog. What breed is she that she does not have a tail?" the announcer asked.

"She is an Australian Shepherd, an American breed, but we had her sent over from Australia," Buster explained.

"Well, she is the best rider on four legs I've ever seen!" said the announcer, and again the crowd cheered loudly.

Winter bounded out to Buster, and the announcer presented her with a large blue rosette. He placed it on her fluffy white chest.

Winter tilted her head to try and see the rosette, and the crowd went even wilder than before.

Chapter Seven

As they left the arena, Buster waving to the crowd, Winter noticed the group of dogs near the gate again. She cringed a little, worried about what they would say to her, if they would laugh at her big blue rosette.

Instead, as she got closer, they all lay down in the sand. Winter didn't know what they were doing. She stopped near them as Buster kept walking.

The brown dog who had laughed the most got up and said, "I am sorry. We were very mean to you."

Another dog got up and looked at Winter. "I wish I didn't have a tail so I could ride like that!"

Winter giggled. She walked back to the truck, promising the other dogs to see them at the next competition.

The other dogs were amazed by her, and each said how much they would love to make it up to her and be her friend.

Winter got back to Old Blue and showed him her rosette. Old Blue nudged her and Winter smiled.

"A problem shared, is a problem halved", Old Blue said to Winter.
"I am always here for you my friend."

Winter was so happy that she had a friend like Old Blue.

Winter

Look out for these other books in the Tales of Tails series

Stories based on real animals, teaching children about kindness and compassion

Visit
www.talesoftailsbooks.com

www.ingramcontent.com/pod-product-compliance
Lightning Source LLC
Chambersburg PA
CBHW042052290426
44110CB00001B/38